# Leonardo da Vinci

John Malam

Heinemann
LIBRARY

**www.heinemann.co.uk/library**
Visit our website to find out more information about **Heinemann** books.

To order:
☎ Phone 44 (0) 1865 888112
🖷 Send a fax to 44 (0) 1865 314091
🖳 Visit the Heinemann Bookshop at **www.heinemann.co.uk/library** to browse our catalogue and order online.

Heinemann Library is an imprint of **Pearson Education Limited**, a company incorporated in England and Wales having its registered office at Edinburgh Gate, Harlow, Essex, CM20 2JE – Registered company number: 00872828 Heinemann is a registered trademark of Pearson Education Limited.

Text © Pearson Education Limited 2009
First published in hardback in 2009
The moral rights of the proprietor have been asserted.

Edited by Louise Galpine and Catherine Clarke
Designed by Kimberly R. Miracle, Jennifer Lacki and Betsy Wernert
Original illustrations © Pearson Education Limited 2008, Illustrated by Mapping Specialists
Picture research by Hannah Taylor
Originated by Modern Age
Printed in China by Leo Paper Group

ISBN 978-0-431-04483-5 (hardback)
13 12 11 10 09
10 9 8 7 6 5 4 3 2

**British Library Cataloguing in Publication Data**
Malam, John, 1957–
Leonardo da Vinci. - (Levelled biographies)
709.2
A full catalogue record for this book is available from the British Library.

**Acknowledgments**
We would like to thank the following for permission to reproduce photographs: © AKG-images pp. **5**, **23** (Nimatallah/Gabinetto Disegni e Stampe); © Alamy p. **7** (Arco Images); © AP Photo p. **13** (Ken Bizzigotti); © Corbis p. **26** (epa/Lydie); © Galleria degli Uffizi, Florence, Italy p. **10** (The Bridgeman Art Library); © Palazzo Medici-Riccardi, Florence, Italy p. **11** (The Bridgeman Art Library); © Photo Scala, Florence p. **17** (2005/The Art Resource); © Robert Harding Picture Library p. **20** (Patrick Dieudonne); © The Art Resource p. **27** (The Andy Warhol Foundation for the Visual Arts/Andy Warhol); © The Bridgeman Art Library pp. **9** (Museo Nazionale del Bargello, Florence, Italy), **14** (Bibliotheque de l'Institut de France, Paris, France), **16** (Bibliotheque de l'Institut de France, Paris, France, Alinari), **18** (Santa Maria della Grazie, Milan, Italy), **19** (Louvre, Paris, France, Giraudon), **21** (Louvre, Paris, France), **25** (Musée de la Ville de Paris, Musée du Petit-Palais, France); © The Science Photo Library p. **4** (Sheila Terry); © V&A Images p. **15**.

Cover photograph of self-portrait of Leonardo da Vinci in red chalk reproduced with permission of © Science Photo Library.

We would like to thank Nancy Harris for her invaluable help in the preparation of this book.

Every effort has been made to contact copyright holders of material reproduced in this book. Any omissions will be rectified in subsequent printings if notice is given to the publishers.

**Disclaimer**
All the Internet addresses (URLs) given in this book were valid at the time of going to press. However, due to the dynamic nature of the Internet, some addresses may have changed, or sites may have changed or ceased to exist since publication. While the author and publishers regret any inconvenience this may cause readers, no responsibility for any such changes can be accepted by either the author or the publishers.

# CONTENTS

Some words are shown in bold, **like this**. You can find out what they mean by looking in the glossary.

# A BORN GENIUS

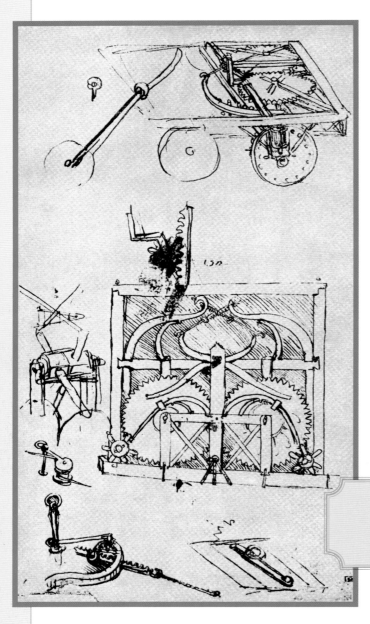

This sketch shows a design for a self-propelled cart. Leonardo drew this around 1480.

Leonardo da Vinci lived more than 500 years ago. He lived in Italy. He was a clever person and was interested in science, buildings, and machines. He was also interested in inventions and art. Leonardo wanted to know as much as he could about his favourite subjects.

He lived long before helicopters, cars, bicycles, and battle tanks. These were machines of the future. Leonardo thought of them all, hundreds of years before they were built.

## A great artist

As an artist, Leonardo was the greatest painter of his day. His picture the *Mona Lisa* is one of the world's most famous paintings.

A few years after Leonardo died, an Italian artist called Giorgio Vasari wrote a book about great artists. Vasari wrote about Leonardo. He said that Leonardo was a genius, which is how we remember him today.

### Renaissance man

"Renaissance" refers to a time in European history. It happened between about 1300 and 1600. That was about 400 to 700 years ago. During this time important steps were taken in art, books, and science. Leonardo was a Renaissance man. This was because of his many interests and talents.

This is a self-**portrait** of Leonardo, aged about 60.

# LEONARDO'S EARLY LIFE

Leonardo was born in Vinci, a village in Italy. His grandfather, Antonio, made a note of his grandson's birth. He wrote: "1452. There was born to me a grandson, the son of Ser Piero my son, on the 15th day of April, a Saturday … He bears the name Leonardo."

Leonardo's father, Piero, was a lawyer. His mother was Caterina, a **peasant** woman. At this time, it would have been unthinkable for Piero to marry a woman from such a poor background.

Soon after Leonardo was born, Piero and Caterina went their separate ways. Piero spent most of his time in Florence, where he lived and worked.

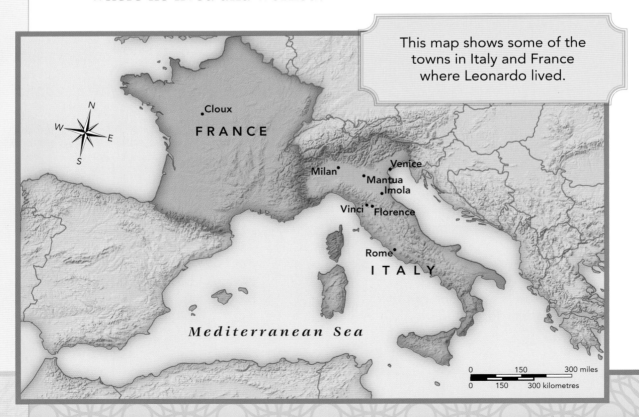

This map shows some of the towns in Italy and France where Leonardo lived.

This is Vinci today. In Leonardo's time there were fewer houses and they were smaller.

## Farm life

Leonardo was brought up by his grandparents, Antonio and Lucia. He was given a basic education, and helped on the family farm. When he was 12 or 13, his grandfather died. From then on, his father took charge of him.

### Lessons learned

Leonardo learned to read and write in Italian. He also learned arithmetic (maths). He may have been taught at home by his grandfather.

## Moving to Florence

Leonardo was about 14 when his father sent for him. The year was 1466. Leonardo travelled to the city of Florence. His father worked there as a lawyer for the Medici family. They were the most important family in Florence.

## Time for learning

Soon after Leonardo arrived, his father realized that Leonardo was talented. He took him to a well known artist called Andrea del Verrocchio. Leonardo went to live at Verrocchio's workshop with other boys. Verrocchio was the teacher, and the boys were his **apprentices**. He trained them to be artists.

## Practising painter

Leonardo did small jobs at first, such as looking after the workshop chickens. Verrocchio taught him to make brushes and paints, and then how to draw and paint. Sometimes, Leonardo was allowed to finish paintings that Verrocchio had started.

In 1472, aged 20, his training ended, and Leonardo became a "*dipintore*". This is Italian for "practising painter". From then on he could work for himself as an artist.

### Why chickens?
Artists kept chickens to lay eggs. Egg yolk was mixed with pigments (colours) and water. The yolk worked like glue, stopping the pigments from separating.

Verrocchio made this metal figure. It might show Leonardo when he was about 14.

# "I DESPAIR"

To succeed as an artist, Leonardo needed a **patron**. Few people in Florence could afford works of art. Those that could, gave work to a few artists they knew. The Medici family could afford to be patrons. Leonardo was a good artist, but he was just one of many looking for work.

This is believed to be a self-portrait of Leonardo when he was about 29.

## A change of luck

Leonardo's luck changed in 1478. He was asked by the city
**officials** (people in charge) to paint a picture of the Nativity
(birth of Christ). It was for the **Chapel** (small building used
for praying) of San Bernardo in Florence. Leonardo started the
picture but never finished it. He was offered more work, but
again he gave up part way through. No one knows if he lost
interest, or was not happy with the work he had done.

The word "*dispero*" is Italian for "I despair". Leonardo scribbled
the word in a notebook. He perhaps felt forgotten by the city's
major patrons, the Medicis.

### The Medici family
The Medici family
earned their money from
banking. They were the
richest family in Florence,
and they ruled the city.

This is a portrait of Lorenzo
de' Medici. He was the
head of the Medici family.

# A NEW BEGINNING

Lorenzo de' Medici was the head of the Medici family. When he found out that Leonardo had made a silver **lyre** (stringed musical instrument) in the shape of a horse's head, he formed a plan. In about 1482, he sent Leonardo and his lyre to Ludovico Sforza. Sforza was the ruler of the city of Milan, in northern Italy. The lyre was a gift from one powerful family to another. It was a sign of their friendship.

## Leonardo's plan

Leonardo also had a plan. Soon after he arrived in Milan, Leonardo wrote to Sforza. He told him that he could build bridges, weapons, and war machines. He wanted Sforza to give him work as an army **engineer**, not as an artist. Engineers were in charge of buildings and machines. Leonardo's plan did not work.

In 1489, after waiting eight years, Sforza gave him a job. It was to make a statue of a horse. It was another project Leonardo did not finish. This time it was because the bronze metal he needed was turned into weapons for war.

### Giant horse
Leonardo planned to make his horse statue 7 metres (23 feet) tall!

Leonardo's huge bronze horse was finally made in 1999. This was more than 500 years after he had designed it.

# LEONARDO'S NOTEBOOKS

While he was in Milan, Leonardo began to write in notebooks. He filled 20,000 pages. He sketched ideas for inventions, from stone-firing **catapults** (weapons) to flapping wings. There is even a drawing of a man using floats to walk on water! Some pages are filled with drawings of faces and body parts. Other pages show designs for bridges and buildings. Many of Leonardo's drawings were rough sketches, but others were carefully drawn and detailed.

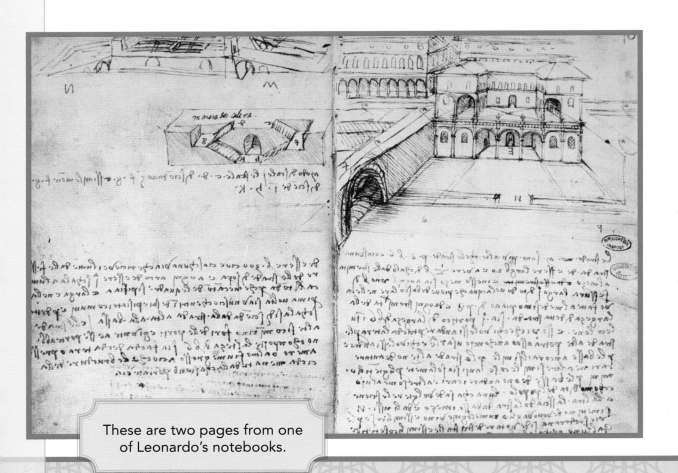

These are two pages from one of Leonardo's notebooks.

## New ideas

Leonardo constantly asked questions about the world around him. He wrote in his notebooks about what he had found. He studied the flight of birds. This helped him with his ideas for flying machines.

Leonardo studied streams, rivers, and the sea. From this came ideas for a water-powered saw. Leonardo was so interested in water that he used 64 different words to describe it!

### "Mirror writing"

Leonardo wrote backwards, from right to left across the page. When looked at in a mirror, it can be read from left to right, as normal. He was left-handed, so it was easier to write from right to left.

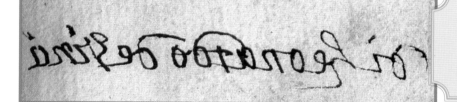

This photo shows Leonardo's actual signature, written from right to left.

This is the same signature, when looked at in a mirror. It reads from left to right.

## The inventor

Leonardo's notebooks contain ideas for hundreds of different inventions. Perhaps his flying machines are the most amazing. To discover the secret of flight, Leonardo studied the wings of birds. This helped him come up with ideas for wings that a person could flap. They were made from wood and linen. He also had an idea for an "aerial screw". This screw would spin round and round, lifting off from the ground. The screw worked in the same way a helicopter does today.

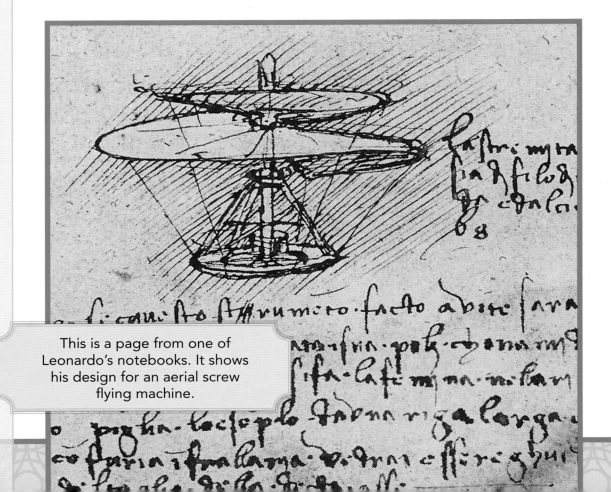

This is a page from one of Leonardo's notebooks. It shows his design for an aerial screw flying machine.

This model of the aerial screw is made from one of Leonardo's designs.

## All in the mind

Leonardo's flying machine, battle tank, submarine, and self-propelled cart (similar to a motor car) existed in his mind. They were also sketches in his notebooks. He may have built models to test his ideas. We do not know if he actually built any of his machines.

### Did Leonardo fly?

Leonardo hints in his notebooks that he was planning to **launch** himself off a building in Milan. He was going to fly off on a wing like a hang-glider. He changed his mind and said it would be better to fly over a lake. He would put a lifebelt around his waist. Did he do it? No, but the thought crossed his mind!

# LEONARDO THE ARTIST

Leonardo's everyday work was as an artist. He mainly painted **portraits** of people, and scenes from the **Bible**. But Leonardo was different from other artists. His pictures of people seem lifelike because of the way he asked them to sit. Before Leonardo, artists painted people as if they were looking straight ahead or to the side. Leonardo painted people with their heads slightly turned.

## Last Supper

Leonardo painted the *Last Supper* on the wall of a **monastery** (place where monks live) in Milan. Instead of using water-based paints, he tried oil paints. It took him three years, and the result was a **masterpiece**. But the paint flaked as it dried. Within 20 years the painting had lost much of its colour.

One of Leonardo's most famous paintings is called *Last Supper*. It shows Jesus Christ sharing bread and wine with his followers.

## Mona Lisa

Leonardo's most famous portrait is called the *Mona Lisa* ("My Lady Lisa"). It is probably of Lisa Gherardini, the wife of an Italian cloth **merchant** (trader). Although Leonardo spent about four years painting this picture, he never felt it was finished.

The *Mona Lisa* is kept at the Louvre Museum in Paris. Leonardo painted this picture in oil paint on a panel of wood.

### Stolen!

The *Mona Lisa* was stolen from the Louvre Museum in 1911. The painting was missing for two years.

# LEONARDO AND SCIENCE

To Leonardo, the world was full of mysteries. For example, he found seashells high up in the mountains. He wondered how they had got there. He knew that most people believed the shells had been washed there by the flood described in the **Bible**. Leonardo dared to question this belief. He came up with an answer of his own. He said the seabed had been pushed up to make the mountains, taking the seashells with it.

Leonardo found seashells in the mountains. He came up with his own ideas about how they got there.

## The human body

Leonardo wanted to understand how the human body worked. He cut up dead bodies to find out. He made drawings of bones, muscles, and **vital organs**. Many of his notebook drawings show shapes and sizes of body parts. They include arms, legs, and noses.

Leonardo asked questions and found out lots of facts. This is how a scientist works.

### Notes on noses

*"Of noses there are ten types: straight, crooked, bent, jutting above or below the midpoint, hawk noses, regular, flat, round, and pointed."*

Leonardo wrote this in one of his notebooks.

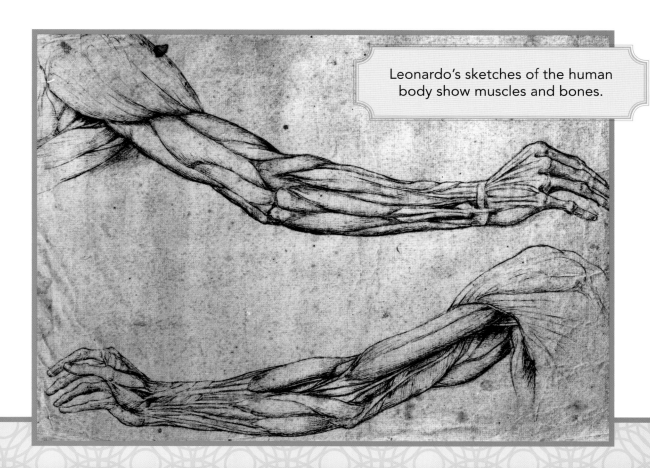

Leonardo's sketches of the human body show muscles and bones.

# FRIENDS AND WORK

Leonardo set up workshops of his own. The first was in Florence in about 1477. Then he set one up in Milan in about 1482. **Apprentices** came to live and work with him. He taught them how to paint. Some stayed with Leonardo only a few months. Others became friends and stayed with him for many years. One of his best friends was nicknamed Salai.

## The new apprentice

Leonardo made a note of when Salai came to live at his workshop in Milan. It was 22 July 1490. Salai was 10 years old. The boy's real name was Giacomo, but "Salai" ("Little Devil") suited him better. Leonardo described Salai as a thief, a liar, and greedy. These were harsh words, but Leonardo had good reason to write them. Salai stole pens from other apprentices, and a purse from a visitor. Despite all this, Leonardo was very fond of Salai.

### Salai and the sweets

Salai pinched a piece of leather that Leonardo was going to use to make a pair of boots. The boy sold the leather, and used the money to buy sweets!

This is one of Leonardo's sketches. It is believed that the young man here is based on Salai.

## No longer safe

In 1499, the city of Milan was **captured** by the French army. It was no longer safe for Leonardo to stay in the city. He left to travel around Italy with Salai. Leonardo accepted many offers of work. He worked as a military **engineer**, strengthening the walls around towns. He also made a bird's-eye-view of Imola, showing the city's streets. This is probably the first street map of a town.

## His final years

After seven years, Leonardo returned to Milan. He was given work by the city's French rulers. In 1516 Leonardo, Salai, and another friend called Francesco Melzi, moved to the town of Cloux in France. Leonardo moved there because he had become artist to the King of France, François I.

As well as working for the king, Leonardo planned to write out the ideas in his notebooks neatly. But he became ill, and on 2 May 1519, Leonardo died aged 67. According to one story, Leonardo died in the arms of King François I.

### Salai and Melzi

Leonardo's friends went home to Italy. Melzi took charge of Leonardo's notebooks. Salai looked after some of his paintings, including the *Mona Lisa*.

This painting by an artist called Ingres shows Leonardo dying in the arms of King François I.

# WHAT LEONARDO LEFT BEHIND

Leonardo da Vinci was a scientist, inventor, and artist. He was an **engineer** who designed machines. He was an **architect** who designed buildings. He lived during a time of new beginnings, new challenges, and new ideas. The Renaissance was the birth of modern Europe.

## Questions and answers

Leonardo worked like a scientist. First, he identified a problem by asking a question. Then, he used his own experiences to make up his own mind, rather than taking the word of others.

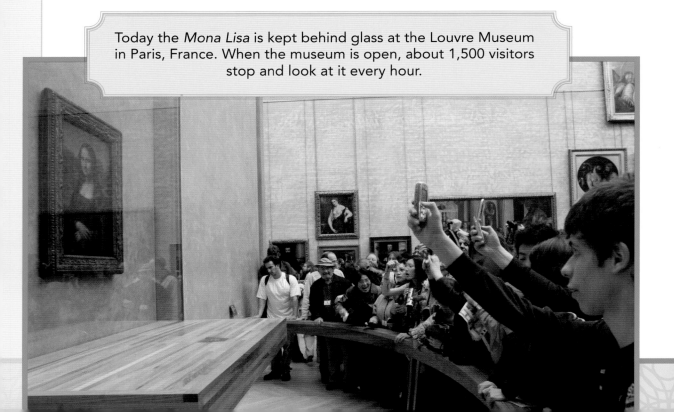

Today the *Mona Lisa* is kept behind glass at the Louvre Museum in Paris, France. When the museum is open, about 1,500 visitors stop and look at it every hour.

## Nothing is impossible

Leonardo's sketches show us that he was full of imagination. He was a great inventor. He imagined flying machines centuries before one was ever built. You can almost hear him saying: "Nothing is impossible." It was as if he could see the future. This is one reason why we think of him as a genius.

Modern artists have used the *Mona Lisa* in their own work. This picture is by Andy Warhol.

### Leonardo's work

- 13 paintings done on his own

- 7 paintings done with others

- 4,000 drawings

- c.20,000 notebook pages (many of these no longer exist)

- hundreds of inventions

# TIMELINES

## Leonardo's life

| | |
|---|---|
| **15 APRIL 1452** | Leonardo is born, at Vinci, Italy |
| c. **1465** | Leonardo's grandfather, Antonio, dies |
| c. **1466** | Leonardo joins the workshop of Andrea del Verrocchio in Florence |
| c. **1477** | Leonardo sets up his own workshop in Florence |
| c. **1482** | Leonardo moves to Milan, to work for Ludovico Sforza. Leonardo begins his scientific studies and starts to write his notebooks. |
| **1489** | Leonardo is asked to make a giant bronze **statue** of a horse |
| **1489** | Leonardo begins to study the human body |
| **1490** | 10-year-old Salai comes to live in Leonardo's workshop |
| **1495** | Leonardo begins to paint the *Last Supper*, on the wall of a **monastery** in Milan |
| **1499** | Leonardo leaves Milan |
| **1502** | Leonardo becomes military **engineer** to Cesare Borgia |
| **1503** | Leonardo begins to paint the *Mona Lisa* |
| **1504** | Leonardo's father dies |
| **1507** | Leonardo becomes artist to King Louis XII of France, based in Milan |
| **1516** | Leonardo becomes artist to King François I of France. He moves to Cloux, France. |
| **2 MAY 1519** | Leonardo dies at Cloux, aged 67 |

# World timeline

| | |
|---|---|
| **1453** | The end of the Hundred Years' War between England and France |
| **1469** | Lorenzo de' Medici becomes ruler of Florence |
| **1475** | The artist Michelangelo Buonarroti is born |
| **1481** | Ludovico Sforza becomes ruler of Milan |
| **1485** | The Tudor **dynasty** begins in England |
| **1492** | Christopher Columbus sails from Spain to the New World (America) |
| **1497** | John Cabot sails from England to Newfoundland |
| **1498** | Vasco da Gama reaches India by sailing around the Cape of Good Hope, southern Africa |
| **1502** | The first watch is made |
| **1508** | Michelangelo begins painting the ceiling of the Sistine Chapel, Rome |
| **1512** | Nicholas Copernicus writes that the Earth circles the Sun |
| **1519** | Ferdinand Magellan begins the first round-the-world trip |

# GLOSSARY

**apprentice** someone who works for another person, and is trained to do that person's job

**architect** person who designs buildings

**Bible** holy book of the Christian religion

**capture** take a person or place, usually by force

**catapult** weapon for throwing stones or bolts

**chapel** small building used for worship (praying)

**engineer** person in charge of machines or engines

**genius** extremely intelligent (clever) person

**launch** send out forcefully. Rockets are launched into the air.

**lyre** u-shaped musical instrument with strings

**masterpiece** great work by an artist

**merchant** person who buys and sells goods

**monastery** place where monks live and work

**official** important person who is in charge of something

**patron** person who gives work to an artist

**peasant** poor person

**portrait** picture of a person

**statue** figure of a person or an animal, usually made from stone or metal

**submarine** type of boat that can move under water

**vital organs** important parts of the body such as the heart, lungs, liver, and kidneys

# Want to know more?

## Books

*Leonardo Da Vinci and His Super-brain*, Michael Cox (Scholastic Hippo, 2003)

*Leonardo Da Vinci: Young Artist, Writer, and Inventor*, George Edward Stanley (Aladdin Paperbacks, 2005)

*The Life and Work of Leonardo da Vinci*, Sean Connolly (Heinemann Library, 2006)

*Who Was Leonardo da Vinci?*, Roberta Edwards (Grosset & Dunlap, 2005)

## Websites

*www.mos.org/leonardo*
A resource for teachers and students developed by the Museum of Science, Boston, USA. There are some great facts such as Leonardo was a vegetarian who loved animals.

*www.museoscienza.org/english/leonardo*
The Leonardo da Vinci Museum of Science and Technology, Milan, Italy. If you can't make it all the way to Milan, take a virtual tour of the museum on the website.

*www.universalleonardo.org*
Find out more about Leonardo's work, whilst making a Leonardo monster sketch and making the Mona Lisa smile!

## Places to visit

*Drumlanrig Castle*, Dumfries and Galloway, Scotland
A chance to see Leonardo's painting The Madonna With The Yarnwinder, which was stolen by thieves in 2003, and which has now been returned.

*Leonardo da Vinci Museum of Science and Technology*, Milan, Italy
A chance to see several models and accurate reconstructions of the machines that Leonardo da Vinci designed while he lived in Milan and throughout his life.

*Louvre Museum*, Paris, France
To see the famous Mona Lisa painting.

*The National Gallery*, Trafalgar Square, London
There are lots of beautiful examples of Leonardo's work here.

# INDEX